THEN & NOW

WHEELING

OPPOSITE: One of the oldest known photographs of Wheeling, this 1852 daguerreotype offers a stunning view of the suspension bridge during one of the countless Ohio River floods that have plagued the city since its founding. This haunting image was captured from the top of the hill behind Lincoln School, a feat made possible only because the hills surrounding Wheeling were essentially deforested in the 19th century. Today trees block this precise view. (Brown collection, Ohio County Public Library.)

THEN & NOW

WHEELING

Seán Patrick Duffy
and Paul Rinkes

For Amina and Patricia—then, now, and always.
And for the Wheeling Area Historical Society, in memory of Dr. Edward Wolf.

Copyright © 2010 by Seán Patrick Duffy and Paul Rinkes
ISBN 978-0-7385-8593-2

Library of Congress Control Number: 2009942517

Published by Arcadia Publishing
Charleston, South Carolina

Printed in the United States of America

For all general information contact Arcadia Publishing at:
Telephone 843-853-2070
Fax 843-853-0044
E-mail sales@arcadiapublishing.com
For customer service and orders:
Toll-Free 1-888-313-2665

Visit us on the Internet at www.arcadiapublishing.com

ON THE FRONT COVER: Here is a view looking east across the historic suspension bridge from Virginia Street on Wheeling Island toward Tenth Street downtown. Built in 1849, the bridge was a remarkable feat of engineering and remains Wheeling's most recognizable landmark. The pedestrians in the 1886 view probably paid a penny toll to cross. (Then, Brown collection, Ohio County Public Library; Now, Paul Rinkes.)

ON THE BACK COVER: In this image looking west down Sixteenth Street from near the Chapline Street intersection during the flood of 1907, the 1859 Wheeling Custom House (now known as West Virginia Independence Hall) can be seen at right, and the Baer and Sons Building (built in 1894), with a water tower, is at left in the distance. They are the only buildings in the photograph still standing. (Dr. Dennis Niess.)

CONTENTS

ACKNOWLEDGMENTS

Thank you to everyone who generously shared their wonderful historic photographs of Wheeling and/or invaluable information for this project, notably: Debra Basham of the West Virginia Archives; Joe Belancic and Fitzsimmons Laws Offices; Megan Clark, curator of the Museums of Oglebay Institute; Joe Coleman and Coleman's Fish Market; Mary Eleanor Colvin; Albert Doughty Jr.; Ellen Dunable; Sr. Joanne Gonter of Mount de Chantal Archives; Ted Hess and Elks Lodge No. 28; Blondine Klimach, Tim Pecsenye, and Wolfgang Wengler of the Nord-Amerikanischer Sängerbund for information on the 1906 Saengerfest; Jeff Knierim; Pete Mamakos; Paul McGinnis; Tim McKormick, Joe Tysk, Mike Panas, and Bob Triveri of Donnie Shell's Bomb Squad; Denis McMorrow, John Osmianski, and Jodi Parsons of La Belle Nail Company; Ron Miller; Linda Endres of the NFL Network; the Ohio County Public Library (OCPL); Craig O'Leary of the Regional Economic Development Partnership; Thaddeus Podratsky; Ryan Rutkowski, archivist for the Diocese of Wheeling-Charleston; the estate of Sarah Ann Ryder; Kathryn M. Snead; Ryan Stanton; Jack Syphers and Augie Oglinsky; Ann Thomas; Mark Thomas and Charlie Schlegel of Ye Olde Alpha; Gary Timmons; Joan Weiskircher of the West Virginia Northern Community College Alumni Association; and the Wheeling National Heritage Area Corporation (WNHAC), including Hydie Friend, Jeremy Morris, Rebekah Karelis, and Chris Villamagna.

Thanks also to Linda Scott of the Northern Regional Juvenile Center (formerly Lincoln School), Montani Towers, and WesBanco for roof and walkway access.

Very special thanks go to Margaret Brennan, Dr. Jeanne Finstein, Dr. David Javersak, and Kate Quinn for proofing the text for historical accuracy. They did their best with limited time. Any remaining errors are ours alone.

Special thanks also to Linda Comins of the *Wheeling Intelligencer and News-Register* for her invaluable help in getting the word out to those with photographs to share.

Many thanks go to the Wheeling Coffee Shoppe, Centre Cup Coffee, Worlds Best Cookie, and the Lebanon Bakery for being there. Please stay.

Thanks to Paul's lovely wife, Amina, for putting up with the hours (and miles) he had to spend to make this project a success.

Finally, our deepest gratitude is reserved for Dr. Dennis Niess, who understands that our history belongs to all of us. This project truly would not have been possible without his generosity and support.

Unless otherwise noted, all modern images were taken by Paul Rinkes.

INTRODUCTION

According to archeologist Delf Norona, Wheeling, Virginia, took its name from the Delaware Indians, who called it Wilunk or Wiilin, meaning "Place of the Head," referencing the scalping and decapitation of a luckless white trespasser and the impaling of his head on a pole at the mouth of the creek.

Despite the rather unwelcoming origin of its name, Wheeling calls itself the "Friendly City" and has been known as a "Gateway to the West" since the convergence of the Ohio River, the National Road, and the Baltimore and Ohio Railroad made it a transportation hub, with the suspension bridge providing access to Ohio and points west.

Wheeling was founded in the late 18th century by Ebenezer Zane, and its frontier legends are plentiful. Fort Henry saw some of the last action of the American Revolution, when Zane's sister Betty made a courageous dash for gunpowder to allow those in the fort to hold out against a siege by British Rangers and their Native American allies. Maj. Samuel McColloch made a daring leap on horseback from the peak of Wheeling Hill to escape hostile natives. And then there is Lewis Wetzel, the ruthless "Deathwind," who waged a lifelong campaign of vengeance against Native Americans.

During the Civil War, Wheeling played host to a series of Unionist conventions that eventually resulted in the birth of the new state of West Virginia, with Wheeling serving for a time as the capital.

Unfortunately, Wheeling's exciting frontier history (as well as much of its Civil War–era history) predated the photographic record, the best of which preserves images of the town during its industrial heyday. Wheeling's transportation advantages, combined with rich supplies of natural resources like coal and iron ore, attracted heavy industry and the vices that accompany it. From the mid-19th through the mid-20th centuries, Wheeling forged iron, steel, nails, wire, glass, tile, and pottery, while entrepreneurs kept working men happy with ample supplies of beer, cigars, and numerous other distractions. The prevalence of industry and vice rendered old Wheeling a grimy, sooty, smelly place—conditions often tangible in the photographs from the period.

The abundance of industrial jobs attracted both African American migrants from the post–Civil War South and emigrants from Germany and Ireland, and later Eastern Europe, Italy, and Lebanon, among other places. The contributions of these migrants and immigrants permanently changed the face of Wheeling, and those changes are also often tangible in the photographs contained in this volume.

A popular destination for German immigrants throughout the 19th century, Wheeling was home to 11 German singing societies. The city played host to three regional Saengerfests (gala gatherings of such singing societies) in 1860, 1885, and 1906. Wheeling businessman Louis F. Stifel was president of the August 1906 festival, which was hosted by the Arion, Beethoven, and Mozart singing societies. The performances, primarily staged at the Court Theatre, drew more than 4,000 visitors to Wheeling, inspiring the *Intelligencer* to proclaim Saengerfest the "greatest musical event in the history of Wheeling." Research indicates that a member of the Stifel family photographed the parade that concluded the 1906

Saengerfest, and a series of those rare, previously unpublished photographs are included in this book through the generosity of Dr. Dennis Niess.

In addition to the rare Saengerfest photographs, the book contains several other previously unpublished looks at historic Wheeling, in addition to numerous familiar images.

Rather than divide the book by subject or function, such as schools, businesses, parks, and so on, as is typically done, this book has been formatted in geographical sequence and includes directions to each site along the way. This will enable readers to follow the trail and visit and read about each "Then & Now" site. It is, in essence, a photographic tour of historic Wheeling from Oglebay Park through Warwood; North Wheeling; Downtown; East, Center, and South Wheeling; and east on National Road through Woodsdale, Pleasant Valley, Elm Grove, and Triadelphia.

Although sincere efforts were made to achieve balance, it simply was not possible to include everything. Limitations of space, unavailability of historic images, and the impossibility of reproducing certain angles due to impediments such as trees and man-made structures that have arisen in the interim decades forced the regrettable but unavoidable omission of numerous desirable images. We hope what remains, while less than comprehensive, still manages to be fairly representative while adding something interesting to the ongoing interpretation of Wheeling's rich history. In other words, if something you hold dear was omitted, we sincerely apologize.

The process of photographing Wheeling's now vacant and decaying landmarks—places once so vital and bustling with activity—and finding empty lots where beautiful edifices once stood was an emotionally draining one. Many unhappy ghosts were encountered. One of our hopes for this book is that it will help increase awareness of what Wheeling once had, what it has lost, and what is still worth fighting to preserve. Perhaps this little picture book will, in its own small way, inspire a few more people to think before they destroy.

In *The Tempest*, William Shakespeare wrote, "Whereof what's past is prologue, what to come, in yours and my discharge;" an appropriate quote for this kind of project.

What has happened in Wheeling's past certainly has changed its present, as the photographs and text that follow make clear. What is to come? That decision belongs to you, and to me, and to its residents. Wheeling's history is beautiful and compelling; in 100 years, we hope the authors who might undertake this project again can say the same things about the decisions being made today.

DOWN RIVER ROAD
AND MAIN STREET

Edwin and Tom Wickham opened this Independent Grocers Association (IGA) store on the southwest corner of Warwood Avenue and North Twenty-fifth Street in 1925. Well regarded for the superior service evidenced by their motto, "It pays to treat the people right," the Wickhams supplied passing riverboats and barges and delivered groceries throughout Warwood. This location remained open until 1972. It is now an empty lot. (Dr. Dennis Niess.)

This trek through Wheeling's past and present begins at beautiful Oglebay Park, where the regal Oglebay Institute Mansion Museum began life as a simple farmhouse built by Hanson and Elizabeth Sprigg Chapline in 1846. Brewer George W. Smith (see page 64) bought the property in 1856, renaming it Waddington Farm. It was purchased in 1900 by industrialist Earl W. Oglebay, who, upon his death in 1926, left his 750-acre farm to the city of Wheeling to be used as a park. The farmhouse, shown here in the late 19th century, underwent numerous changes over the years and now houses a fine collection of local archival materials. (Museums of Oglebay Institute.)

Turn right on Route 88, left onto Pogue Run Road, right onto Ohio County Highway 7, left onto Table Rock Lane, left onto Cherry Hill Road, and left on West Virginia Route 2. Drive to 1609 Warwood Avenue, where Engine Company No. 11 proudly displayed its 750 American La France triple combination engine when this photograph was taken in 1925. Designed by Wheeling architect Millard Fillmore Giesey and built in 1923, the firehouse operated until 1973. Attorney Robert P. Fitzsimmons, whose grandfather served as a volunteer firefighter at No. 11, purchased and renovated the property in 1994 to house his law firm. (*History of Fire Fighting in Wheeling*, 1925, OCPL.)

Continue south on Warwood Avenue, turning right at North Sixth Street. The Warwood Veterans Association Club is a few blocks down on the left. It was from here that, in December 1974, a group of young men journeyed to Pittsburgh's Three Rivers Stadium to root for the Steelers in the playoffs. As they warmed up with beverages and song, an NFL Films cameraman noticed. The footage he captured—and John Facenda's baritone description of them as the "Prophets from Pittsburgh"—would catapult the men into football fandom immortality. "We've got a feeling," they sang, composing the lyrics on the spot, "Pittsburgh's going to the Super Bowl!" The Steelers won that afternoon and went on to win Super Bowl IX a few weeks later. In the 36 years since, the footage has become iconic; it is even in the Pro Football Hall of Fame. Recently, Bob Triveri, Mike Panas, Joe Tysk, and Tim McCormick (from left to right below) reunited outside the Vets Club, where the Steelers' journey began. Tysk still had the hats. (Then, NFL Network; Now, Seán Duffy.)

Follow West Virginia Route 2 down River Road and just into North Wheeling. Established in 1850 by Dr. Simon Hullihen and Bishop Richard V. Whelan, Wheeling Hospital moved to the Sweeney mansion on Main Street in North Wheeling in 1856. The Sisters of St. Joseph, who were called upon to administer the hospital in 1853, cared for sick and wounded soldiers of the Civil War at the North Wheeling location. A North Wing was added in 1903 and a South Wing in 1914. The mansion was demolished in 1928 to make way for a new center building. All three structures can be seen in this photograph from the 1930s. A new hospital was opened in 1975, and this structure was demolished in the late 1990s. Construction of the HOPE VI Housing development, seen in the modern photograph, commenced in 1999. In the distance is the spire of the Church of the Sacred Heart (built in 1904), now an autism treatment center. (Gwinn collection/WNHAC.)

Continue south on Main Street past the historic Henry K. List House, with the statue honoring worker-friendly stogie-maker Augustus Pollack in the yard, to the off-ramp of the Fort Henry Bridge. Opened to traffic in 1955, the 2,270-foot, four-lane, tied-arch bridge was constructed using 6,700 tons of steel and 21,300 cubic yards of concrete. Its piers are sunk into solid rock 40 feet below the river, and its span arch soars 203 feet above the water surface at normal levels. The bridge, seen here under construction in the early 1950s, provides an ultramodern artery for the Old National Pike (U.S. Route 40) into Ohio and stands in stark contrast to its 160-year-old neighbor, the venerable suspension bridge. (Then, Dr. Dennis Niess; Now, Seán Duffy.)

Enter downtown Wheeling and look east from the southwest corner of Tenth and Main Streets. The old Lincoln School (which was segregated) can be seen in the distance in this 1930s photograph. The building on the left was the Hotel Wheeling and now houses the Bridge Tavern and Grill. The No. 19 trolley was an interurban double-sized car that carried passengers, including a young crooner named Dino Paul Crocetti (better known as Dean Martin), north to Steubenville, Ohio. (Gwinn collection/WNHAC.)

Face west at Tenth and Main Streets for a good look at Wheeling's iconic suspension bridge. Designed by engineer Charles Ellet Jr. and built using local materials, the innovative, French-style wire cable structure was—at 1,010 feet—the longest clear span bridge in the world when it opened in 1849. Thousands of spectators cheered as the last plank was hammered onto the bridge deck. The durable bridge survived a devastating 1852 flood and a legal challenge from the City of Pittsburgh only to be badly damaged by an 1854 tornado. It was rebuilt using the same towers and cables and remains the oldest suspension bridge in the country still in use. (Jack Syphers.)

DOWN RIVER ROAD AND MAIN STREET

To get the full flavor of the suspension bridge, it is best to walk across and to consider that, for nearly half a century, the bridge was the only way for residents of the island to get to town short of swimming or floating. Pedestrians were charged a toll to cross. Not surprisingly, the penny toll was wildly unpopular. This late-19th century photograph provides a view east down Tenth Street. (Ellen Dunable.)

This 1913 photograph of the Twelfth-to-Fourteenth Street Wheeling waterfront was probably taken from the old steel bridge, which spanned the Ohio River from 1891 to 1962. But essentially the same view can be had from the suspension bridge. This 1913 photograph shows the Pennsylvania Railroad Station and Wheeling's "skyscraper," the Schmulbach Building (built in 1907). The waterfront is now home to the Wheeling Heritage Port development, a fine riverside venue for festivals and concerts. (Sarah Ann Ryder estate.)

DOWN RIVER ROAD AND MAIN STREET

Follow National Road west into Bridgeport, Ohio, and take Kirkwood Heights to the top of the hill. This breathtaking 1885 view from the summit looking east shows the old wooden covered bridge. Built by the Zanes in 1837, it spanned the back-river from Wheeling Island to Bridgeport. The modern photograph from the same vantage point shows the interesting Victorian steel truss Bridgeport Bridge. Built in 1893 by the Wrought Iron Bridge Company, the bridge is closed to traffic and endangered. (Brown collection, OCPL.)

A clearing a few hundred feet farther south on Kirkwood Heights provided this splendid 1885 view of Wheeling Island, with the suspension bridge and the Wheeling skyline in the distance. (Brown collection, OCPL.)

Retrace the path down from Kirkwood Heights and back into Wheeling over the suspension bridge. Look southwest from Tenth Street. This 1927 view shows the buildings that were razed to make way for the Capitol Theatre, which opened in 1928. The beautiful Beaux-Arts–style theater, designed by architect Charles W. Bates and built by the R. R. Kitchen Company, served as the home of both the Wheeling Symphony and the Jamboree, broadcast on WWVA Radio, before closing its doors in 2007. Happily, after a grassroots effort involving several Wheeling organizations, the Capitol Theatre was purchased by the Wheeling–Ohio County Convention and Visitors Bureau, restored, cleaned by 144 community volunteers, and reopened in September 2009. The recently restored Paxton-Zinn building is also visible at right in both photographs. (Gwinn collection/WNHAC.)

Travel one block south to stand in front of the Stone and Thomas building, and look north for this view of the Capitol Theatre. The fact that Marlene Dietrich and John Wayne are starring in *Seven Sinners* dates the historic photograph to the Christmas season of 1940. The Capitol Theatre offered feature films until the early 1960s. (Gwinn collection/WNHAC.)

Billed as a "Wonderland of Entertainment," the 3,000-seat Capitol Theatre opened its doors on Thanksgiving Day in 1928. Expensive mimosa perfume, supplied by George Stifel Company, permeated the theater as attendees enjoyed performances by dancers, tenor John Steele, a prelude featuring Dusty Rhodes at the "$50,000 Wonder Organ," and the silent film *Romance of the Underworld*, starring Mary Astor. More than 15,000 attended throughout the day. Among them was Mary Eleanor Bowie, age 7. Eight decades later, the Capitol was saved from the wrecking ball and reopened with another gala variety show, and 87-year-old Mary Eleanor Bowie Colvin was back, receiving an enthusiastic round of applause. She was also an honored guest at the Ohio County Public Library's celebratory screening of *Romance of the Underworld*, where this photograph was taken. Of the original event, Colvin remembers little more than the organ prelude and the chorus girls who, because of the lighting, appeared to be dancing in snow. (Then, Eleanor Colvin; Now, Seán Duffy.)

Cross Main Street, travel south half a block, and look north. This five-story structure at 1030 Main Street was built in 1900 to house the Stone and Thomas Department Store, founded by Elijah Stone and Jacob Thomas. Featuring a popular tearoom with a lunch counter on the lower level, Stone's served as one of Wheeling's anchor retail establishments for decades. This is the first in a series of unpublished photographs believed to be of the 1906 Saengerfest, taken by a member of the Stifel family. The banner, written in German, reads "*Wo Ist Der Koenig*" (Where Is the King?), possibly a tribute to Augustus Pollack, the well-regarded maker of Crown Stogies and the president of Wheeling's 1885 Saengerfest, who died a few months before the 1906 festival started. Reporting on the Saengerfest, the *Wheeling Intelligencer* included a similar photograph of the Stone and Thomas building draped with flags, pennants, and bunting. The Stone's building was refurbished in 2007 through the efforts of the Regional Economic Development Partnership and now houses office space for a legal outsourcing company. (Dr. Dennis Niess.)

DOWN RIVER ROAD AND MAIN STREET

At the bottom of Main Street hill at Twelfth Street, look to the northeast corner to see the National Exchange Bank Building (built in 1899). The building on the left, visible in the historic photograph, housed Stifel Dry Goods, which was founded in 1878 by George Stifel. It is now a parking lot. The historic image is the second in a series of previously unpublished photographs of the 1906 Saengerfest. Note the photographer in the foreground. (Then, Dr. Dennis Niess; Now, Seán Duffy.)

Cross Main Street to the northeast corner of Twelfth Street and look east for the third view in the 1906 Saengerfest series. Here parade attendees could enjoy the mysterious French Theater, offering the inexplicable yet intriguing promise of "Parisian Pose Plastic Living Art Models" inside. The top corner of the historic McLure Hotel can be seen in the distance. (Then, Dr. Dennis Niess; Now, Seán Duffy.)

Travel half a block east on Twelfth Street and look back west toward the Ohio River. In this photograph of the area, probably taken during the 1907 flood, the south facade of the National Exchange Bank building can be seen on the right. Across Main Street on the right is the People's Bank Building, which was built in 1870. The stylish National Bank of West Virginia building, constructed in 1915, can be seen on the left in the modern photograph. The bank was designed by Charles W. Bates, who also designed the Capitol Theatre. The gentleman marked with the "X" in the historical photograph is John Niess, grandfather of Dr. Dennis Niess, who shared the photograph. (Dr. Dennis Niess.)

Continue south, stopping at the southeast corner of Fourteenth and Main Streets looking north. This 1953 photograph tells many tales. To the right is a neon sign advertising "Original Dicarlo's Pizza," an Ohio Valley legend. In the distance are the National Bank of West Virginia, the Boury building, and the Ohio Valley Drug Supply Company building. The modern photograph includes a look at the van used to promote the local professional ice hockey team, the Wheeling Nailers. The last of Wheeling's trolley cars were taken off line in 1948 and were replaced by public buses, like the one shown. (Gwinn collection/WNHAC.)

DOWN RIVER ROAD AND MAIN STREET

Continue to the southeast corner of the Sixteenth Street intersection and look north for this interesting view of Main Street. In the 1940s, the view was dominated by the triangular Wheeling Steel and Iron Company headquarters (built in 1904), Wheeling's answer to Manhattan's famous Flatiron Building. The unusual structure still stands, nowadays sharing the block with the Robert C. Byrd Intermodal Transportation Center. Trolley cars started running in Wheeling in 1863 and the first electric cars in 1888. (Gwinn collection/WNHAC.)

Jack Syphers (age 89, standing, and below) and Augustus "Augie" Oglinsky (age 103) were Wheeling's last two living trolley car men when this photograph was taken on October 16, 2009. Syphers started working for Wheeling's Co-Operative Transit Company in 1942 at age 21. He operated trolley cars until they were replaced by buses in 1948. Driving a trolley was no easy task. "The operator had to learn every mile of track and every switch on the system," Syphers said. Oglinsky started with the Wheeling Traction Company in 1923 as a 16-year-old on a pick and shovel crew. He went on to work nearly every job with the company, retiring in 1975 as president and general manager. "Anything broke, you had to repair or replace to make it go," Augie said, "Anything to make it go." (Jack Syphers.)

The 159-foot Main Street Bridge spanning Wheeling Creek near its mouth was the longest single-span stone arch bridge in the United States when it was completed in 1892. During construction, the timber false arch, seen in the photograph, was used to hold the stones in place. More than 3,300 tons of locally quarried stones were used. The *Wheeling Intelligencer* reported that large crowds of people gathered on the temporary bridge daily to watch the construction, ignoring a sign that read, "Danger! No one is allowed to loaf on this bridge by order of the Board of Public Works." But the people gathered "of their own free will and accord," the newspaper joked. The grand opening was a festive occasion featuring speeches by city leaders, a banquet, a keg of beer from Anheuser-Busch, and impromptu races to be the first to cross the new bridge. (Mount de Chantal Archives.)

From the stone bridge, head toward the river and down the steps of the Wheeling Heritage Port Amphitheater for this view of the waterfront, where the old Steel Bridge once stood. Twenty thousand people attended the opening of the steel bridge in October 1891, many crossing and recrossing the 1,819-foot span that the *Wheeling Intelligencer* hailed as "a specimen of enterprise and progressive spirit." The city promised island residents that the new structure, unlike the suspension bridge, would not have pedestrian tolls. The promise was not kept—it also cost a penny to cross. Streetcars also made use of the bridge, which was demolished in 1962. Here ice-skaters enjoy a frozen Ohio River beneath the steel bridge in February 1905. (Ellen Dunable.)

DOWN RIVER ROAD AND MAIN STREET

Head back up the steps toward Water Street in front of the old Windsor Hotel. Look north for this view of the area where the old Pennsylvania Railroad Station once stood. In this well-known photograph, taken during the 1907 flood, a train leaving the station was nearly engulfed by flood waters. The photographer apparently stood on the bow of a riverboat. A ladder was used to duplicate the angle. While the station is long gone, the stone-block ramp that led to it still stands. (Dr. Dennis Niess.)

Look south from the top steps of the amphitheater for this view of the riverfront, long a stop for Ohio River steamboats. The prototype of American steamboats was actually built nearby on Wheeling Creek by Henry Shreve in 1815. This interesting old stereograph (an early 3-D image viewed with special glasses) shows a steamboat docked approximately where the amphitheater is now. Heritage Port is once again friendly to river traffic, offering mooring for festivals, fireworks displays, and other events. Wheeling hosts a Sternwheel Festival at Heritage Port each September. (Dr. Dennis Niess.)

DOWN RIVER ROAD AND MAIN STREET

CHAPTER 2

LOAFING DOWNTOWN

Before it was closed by the landmark U.S. Supreme Court desegregation decision in *Brown v. Board of Education* (decided in 1954), Lincoln School, on Chapline Street hill above Tenth Street, educated Wheeling's African American students from grammar school through high school for nearly a century. Here a group of Lincoln students poses outside the earliest school building around 1885. (Kathryn M. Snead.)

Return to the Main Street stone bridge and make the left onto Sixteenth Street. Take the first sharp right onto South Street and stop a few yards onto the Market Street Bridge. Look north for this interesting view of Market Street, taken during the 1906 Saengerfest. Note that the Schmulbach building (constructed in 1907) is not yet dominating the city's skyline. The Wheeling Custom House (now West Virginia Independence Hall), with its multiple chimneys, can be seen in the distance. The buildings to the right, including the church, were demolished within a year and replaced by the Baltimore and Ohio (B&O) Railroad Depot in 1908. (Then, Dr. Dennis Niess; Now, Seán Duffy.)

Move a few hundred feet north on Market Street for this view similar to the one on page 38 but taken one year later, during the 1907 flood. The freshly minted Schmulbach building can now be seen clearly in the distance. The Wheeling Custom House is again visible, and the clock tower of the old City Building can be seen at right. Note that many of the buildings visible at the right in the 1906 photograph are gone, as the B&O Depot was under construction. (Dr. Dennis Niess.)

As in most river towns, Wheeling's older citizens can mark the time with floods. Travel down Market Street to Sixteenth Street for this look west from near the Chapline Street intersection during the flood of 1907. The Custom House can be seen at right, and the Baer and Sons Building (constructed in 1894), with a water tower, is at left in the distance. The Baers were wholesale grocers and coffee roasters. (Dr. Dennis Niess.)

Although its population has never exceeded 65,000, Wheeling has been home to more than 50 movie theaters and performance halls over the years. One of the most popular, the Liberty, occupied the northwest corner of Sixteenth and Market Streets. The *No, No, Nanette* movie poster dates this photograph to December 1940. The site currently houses a car dealership. (West Virginia State Archives.)

Designed by Ammi B. Young, the Wheeling Custom House was completed in 1859 on the northeast corner of Sixteenth and Market Streets. When Virginia seceded from the Union in 1861, angry delegates from the western counties convened at the customhouse and organized a restored government of Virginia. A constitutional convention followed, and on June 20, 1863, West Virginia was named the 35th state. The customhouse was sold to private interests in 1912 and was greatly altered. Responding to a mid-century grassroots campaign, the state purchased and restored the structure according to Young's original plans. It was reopened as West Virginia Independence Hall in 1979. (Brown collection, OCPL.)

Travel another block north on Market Street to see the original location of the Sears and Roebuck Company department store in Wheeling. The store opened at 1416 Market in 1930, then moved to its more familiar Eleventh Street location in 1941.

The building at right housed Browne Brothers Tailors, an exclusive establishment that served the well dressed of the city, state, and region from 1899 to 1945. (Thaddeus Podratsky.)

To get this aerial view of the Rogers Hotel one must seek permission from WesBanco to access the glass walkway spanning Fourteenth Street. The hotel is a landmark, infamously "fireproof," perpetually abandoned, yet seemingly indestructible, oft sold and resold, at once recognizable and, at the same time, an inexplicable eyesore. Built in 1920, the durable Rogers has been offering $8 air-conditioned rooms with television and a shower for more than half a century. The hotel was designed by architect Edward Bates Franzheim, who also designed the Court Theater. In 1937, when this photograph was taken, the Rogers was among the finest hotels in town. In the background sits the Second United Presbyterian Church, now demolished. (West Virginia State Archives.)

LOAFING DOWNTOWN

Judging by the abundance of available images, the four corners of Fourteenth and Market Streets were among the busiest and most photographed in old Wheeling. The Hub, one of Wheeling's most popular clothiers, hatters, and furnishers, sat on the northeast corner. Founded by S. S. Fridenberg and M. Sonneborn, the Hub served Wheeling from 1891 to 1966. This photograph was taken just after the 1913 flood. The Hub site is now an empty lot. (Sarah Ann Ryder estate.)

Turn to face due west for this stunning view of Fourteenth Street and the Ohio River during the 1907 flood. House and Hermann, a home furnishings store, sat on the southwest corner of the intersection at left. It was destroyed by fire in 1917. The Central Union and Trust Company building was constructed on the site in 1924. In the distance at left is the Henry K. List wholesale grocery building (constructed in 1868), now the Wheeling Artisan Center. On the northwest corner at right sat the Reilly Building (constructed in 1886). WesBanco now stands on the site. (Dr. Dennis Niess.)

LOAFING DOWNTOWN

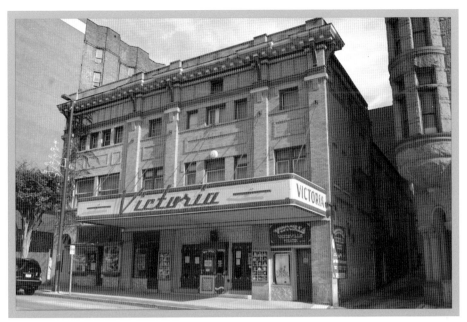

About a block north on the east side of Market Street sits the Victoria, which opened in 1908 as a vaudeville theater. Opening night featured mirror dancer Martynne, along with acrobats and performing dogs, all accompanied by a six-piece orchestra. The founder was George C. Schafer, who named his new theater after a little girl whose father operated a jewelry store near Stone and Thomas. By the late 1930s, when this photograph was taken, the Old Vic was largely a movie theater and would remain one until closing in the 1980s. As of 2010, the Victoria is once again operating as a vaudeville theater under the direction of local showman Earl Brown. (West Virginia State Archives.)

Opened in 1852 on the southeast corner of Market and Twelfth Streets, the McLure is Wheeling's oldest operating hotel. In the early days, the McLure featured a courtyard with hitching posts for horses and a "Ladies'" entrance with wider doors to accommodate hoop skirts. Also famous for its menu, the McLure served venison, tongue, and pig's feet, among other things. The impressive roster of famous guests of the McLure includes U.S. presidents Ulysses S. Grant, Harry S. Truman, and John F. Kennedy, as well as celebrities, including Buffalo Bill Cody, Sarah Bernhardt, and Marilyn Monroe. The hotel served as the forum for Senator Joe McCarthy's infamous speech alleging Communist infiltration of the government. E. M. Statler, the McLure's most successful bellboy, founded what would become the Hilton and Sheraton hotel empires. (Ellen Dunable.)

A block and a half north of the McLure on the left sits the Market Plaza on land donated to the city in 1821 by Noah Zane. The original Market House was built in 1822. It grew to contain 76 stalls and, for a time, housed Wheeling's city hall. Slaves were sold at the Tenth Street end. The old wooden structure was replaced in 1913 by the brick and steel Market Auditorium, pictured here in 1948. Designed by noted architect Frederick Faris, the 64-stall auditorium offered a farmer's market at ground level and a roller-skating rink on the second floor. It was razed in 1964. (Ellen Dunable.)

Walk to the center of Market Plaza and look south. Louis' Famous Hot Dog is a Wheeling institution, the home of one of those iconic and addictive local foods—like Coleman's fish sandwiches and DiCarlo's Pizza. The durable business was founded nine decades ago by a Greek immigrant named Louis Panaotis Mamakos. In 1919, Louis opened a bake shop in a small building on Eleventh and Chapline Streets. He also sold hot dogs for a nickel each. He kept the corner location until 1969, when he opened a new shop a block northwest in the market plaza. Shown here in 1971, the new plaza shop did great business until the Ohio Valley Mall in St. Clairsville was opened in 1978. The Mamakos family opened a hot dog shop in the Elm Terrace Shopping Plaza in Elm Grove in 1981. It is still operating. (Pete Mamakos.)

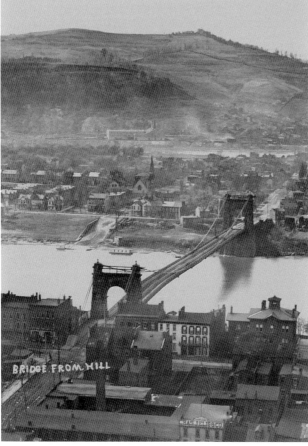

BRIDGE FROM HILL

Continue north on Market Street over Interstate 70 and the entrance to Wheeling Tunnel. At the traffic light on Seventh Street, make a sharp right up a small road called West Chapline Street, a left onto Chapline Street, then a right onto Grandview Street. At the top on the right is an abandoned cul-de-sac called City View Avenue. In its industrial heyday, Wheeling's hills were virtually bereft of trees. Consequently, the hills around the city offered spectacular views like this one, captured in 1885. To get the same view of the bridge today is virtually impossible. Even in the dead of winter, the view is blocked by a tangle of tree branches. The roof of the old Lincoln School (from which the modern photograph was taken) is really the only option, and not a recommended one. (Brown collection, OCPL.)

Head back down the hill and left onto Chapline Street. A few hundred feet down on the left sits the Lincoln School building. Founded in 1866, Lincoln was one of the first public schools in the country for African American students. The building pictured was replaced in 1943. Only the stairs remain. The newer structure, still standing in the area left of the photograph, was designed by architects Frederick and Phillip Faris and was closed in 1956 in the wake of desegregation. It now houses the Northern Regional Juvenile Detention Center. (West Virginia State Archives.)

Born on March 11, 1918, Kathryn Williams Snead graduated with honors from Lincoln School and summa cum laude from Ohio University. A lifelong educator, Snead is one of the last living Lincoln School teachers. She also taught black history at Ohio University Eastern and worked as a tutor for the St. Clairsville, Ohio, school system. Her innovative teaching methods have included portrayals of prominent African American women. She has been honored with the Coretta Scott King and Rosa Parks Awards for her work. Here she is in 1925 while a Lincoln School student and, in more recent times, presenting a program for her grandson Arthur's second-grade class. (Kathryn Snead.)

Travel south on Chapline Street from Lincoln School, stopping at the intersection with Twelfth Street. Built in 1907 on the northwest corner of the intersection, Wheeling's new granite Federal Building and U.S. Courthouse (and post office) was intended to replace the outmoded and undersized 1859 Wheeling Custom House (now Independence Hall) located at Sixteenth and Market Streets. The original section of the Beaux-Arts–neoclassical structure looks essentially the same in both photographs, while a sleek new glass wing was added to the north side of the building in 2004. The Federal Building still looks the part—stately, solid, and dignified. (Mount de Chantal Archives.)

On the southeast corner of Twelfth and Chapline Streets sits the Court Theatre. The city hired architect Edward Bates Franzheim (who designed the Rogers Hotel) to design the Court (also known as the Board of Trade Building), to be constructed in 1901. Franzheim, a great patron of the arts, then served for a time as the Court's manager and even wrote and acted in plays. In its prime, the Court was known as one of the most acoustically perfect theaters in the country. It played host to the singing events of the 1906 Saengerfest, including a rendition of the "Star Spangled Banner" sung by 1,500 people. The Virginia Theater, seen just beyond the Court, was built by Charles Feinler in 1908. Feinler named the theater after his daughter. The Virginia became home to the WWVA *Jamboree* in 1934. Here *Jamboree* patrons stand on line to see the Saturday night show, as Troy Donahue stars in *Parrish* at the Court, around 1961. (West Virginia State Archives.)

Just northeast of the Court Theatre, across Twelfth Street, stands the Twelfth Street Garage, seen here just after it was constructed in 1922 by the R. R. Kitchen Company, the same contractors who would build the Capitol Theatre six years later. The infamous crime boss Bill Lias kept his fleet of cars in this garage. Note the posters advertising the movie *Bonnie Brier Bush* for the nearby Virginia Theatre. (West Virginia State Archives.)

The old Odd Fellows Hall was constructed on the corner of Twelfth and Chapline Streets in 1859. From 1863 to 1870, the building served as temporary quarters for Linsly Military Institute cadets, whose own building was being used as the capitol of the new state of West Virginia. Most of the original Odd Fellows Hall was destroyed by fire in 1950. The corner space is currently occupied by Metropolitan Citi Grill. It is familiar to most Wheeling residents as the longtime site of Elby's Restaurant and later Lanos and Kraus Delicatessen. (Odd Fellows and Gary Timmons.)

Travel south one block to the northeast corner of Fourteenth and Chapline Streets to see this distinctive Federal and Neoclassical Revival–style brick residence built by the Paull family in the 1850s. In 1890, the building was purchased by the Fort Henry Club. Founded for gentlemen of "genteel manners and cultured tastes" during Wheeling's business heyday, the Fort Henry Club was the town's most exclusive retreat for the wealthy. It featured the finest furniture and decor, an opulent ballroom, a renowned taproom, and other amenities for the corporate elite. Celebrity guests included Charles Lindbergh and Herbert Hoover. (*Art Work of Wheeling*, 1904, OCPL.)

A short walk from the Fort Henry Club to the top of the hill across Fourteenth Street from the Rogers Hotel provides this view of the southwest corner of Market and Fourteenth Streets. Designed by architect Charles W. Bates (who also designed the Capitol Theatre), the Central Union Trust Company Building was constructed in 1924 by the R. R. Kitchen Company. It is now owned by WesBanco. The Henry K. List wholesale grocery building (constructed in 1868), now the Wheeling Artisan Center, can be seen to the right of the Central Union building. (West Virginia State Archives.)

Travel south to the northeast corner of Sixteenth and Chapline Streets. In 1875, the argument between Charleston and Wheeling regarding which city should be the permanent capital of the young state turned ugly when the legislature voted to pack up the government and ship it back up river to Wheeling. A Charleston newspaper called the decision a "coup," and the *Wheeling Intelligencer* called Charleston a "one-horse town." Meanwhile, the citizens of Wheeling voted to erect a new state capitol on the corner of Sixteenth and Chapline Streets, and as Charleston threatened "war," a steamboat shipped the government back to Wheeling. Only a decade later, Charleston had the votes to get the "floating capital" back and became the permanent state capital in 1885. The Wheeling building, shown here around 1906, featured a steeple with a 2.5-ton clock. It served as the seat of the city and county governments until it was replaced by the current modernistic structure in 1960. Built in 1866, the historic St. Matthews Episcopal Church can be seen at left in both photographs. (Dr. Dennis Niess.)

GOOSETOWN TO RITCHIETOWN N'AT

John Coleman (pictured over the shoulder of his grandson Joe) founded his now-legendary Wheeling restaurant in 1914 in Stone and Thomas Alley, then moving to the familiar Centre Market location in the early 1920s. John's son Ray took over the family business in 1946. "Probably one of the last things my grandfather did was to come up with the recipe for the seasoning for the fish sandwich," Joe said. Ray started making sandwiches based on his father's recipe, and the legend of Coleman's fish sandwiches grew. Joe runs Coleman's these days, and he is teaching his daughter, Jodie, the business. (Joe Coleman; Seán Duffy.)

Stop a block south of the city building to see the steel-framed American Renaissance–style B&O passenger station, which was built of brick, granite, and limestone in 1908. The building, shown in 1913, featured marble floors, electric elevators, brass chandeliers, and elaborate cast-iron staircases leading to an elevated concourse where trains entered the station from a viaduct over Seventeenth Street. The station also boasted its own power plant across Chapline Street near the current location of the Ohio County Public Library. Passenger service ended in 1962. The beautifully restored building at 1704 Market Street now houses offices and classrooms for West Virginia Northern Community College. (Sarah Ann Ryder estate.)

The south side of the B&O passenger station featured the old Seventeenth Street viaduct that brought trains to the elevated concourse. This area became infamous during the 1970s as a hub of prostitution. The modern photograph reveals some of the renovations performed by West Virginia Northern Community College (WVNCC), including the removal of the decrepit viaduct. (WVNCC Alumni Association.)

George W. Smith opened Wheeling's first brewery in 1812 on the southeast corner of what is now Seventeenth and Chapline Streets. It operated until 1877, when this photograph was taken. In 1890, Flaccus Brothers wholesale grocery purchased the Smith building, operating there until 1905. A year later, the old building was razed and replaced by the Wheeling Warehouse and Storage building, which spanned Seventeenth Street from Eoff Street to Chapline Street. Wheeling Wholesale Grocery Company purchased the building in 1936, and in 2004, West Virginia Northern Community College bought and renovated the structure. It now houses classrooms, laboratories, and a gymnasium. (Then, Albert Doughty Jr.; Now, Seán Duffy.)

Travel east on Sixteenth Street then north on Eoff Street. The second Linsly Institute building was constructed on the northwest corner of Eoff and Fifteenth Streets and was opened in 1859 as the headquarters for the military academy. West Virginia's first governor, Arthur Boreman, was inaugurated on the front lawn on June 20, 1863. The new state rented the building from the academy, using it as the state capitol and forcing the cadets to temporarily relocate to the Odd Fellows Hall on Chapline and Twelfth Streets. When the state government left by riverboat for Charleston in 1870, the building once again functioned as a school until 1927. In 1993, the building was purchased and renovated by local attorney Pat Cassidy, and it now houses his law firm. (Brown collection, OCPL.)

The Order of Elks, an American fraternal and charitable organization, opened its 28th lodge in Wheeling in 1884, the first Elks Lodge in West Virginia. In 1904, Lodge No. 28 purchased and renovated the Neoclassical Revival–style William B. Simpson home at 32 Fifteenth Street, just across from the Linsly Institute Building. The Elks building currently houses a law firm. (*Wheeling 28 B.P.O.E., 100th Anniversary 1884–1984*, Ted Hess, 1984.)

German immigrant Anton Reymann was a successful Wheeling businessman, philanthropist, and brewery owner and Henry Schmulbach's chief rival. Reymann's brewery was located in the Manchester section of East Wheeling, across the Seventeenth Street bridge near Wheeling Corrugating. At its peak, the brewery was one of the largest in West Virginia, churning out 150,000 barrels of beer per year. Reymann built an imposing castle-like mansion on the northeast corner of Fifteenth and Eoff Streets, pictured here in the 1940s. The mansion is now gone, except for the carriage house, which houses Padden Pharmacy. The dome of St. Joseph's Cathedral can be seen in the distance. (Then, Albert Doughty Jr.; Now, Seán Duffy.)

Halfway between Thirteenth and Twelfth
Streets on Eoff Street is the site of Wheeling's
first synagogue, now a parking lot. By
the mid-1840s, Wheeling was home to
Western Virginia's first Jewish settlement,
and Wheeling's L'Shem Shomayim (For
the Sake of Heaven) became the city's
first Jewish congregation. In 1892, the
Wheeling congregation built the Eoff
Street Temple, seen here in 1904. It
was replaced by the Woodsdale Temple,
now Temple Shalom, which was built in
1957 on Bethany Pike. (Then, *Art Work of
Wheeling*, 1904, OCPL; Now, Seán Duffy.)

Travel back to Fifteenth Street, make a left, and proceed to the intersection with Jacob Street. Designed by architect Edward Bates Franzheim (who also designed Court Theatre), the corporate headquarters for Hazel-Atlas Glass Company was constructed on the corner of Fifteenth and Jacob Streets in 1930. The four-story quarter-block building featured a multiton glass entrance with revolving door, art deco–style light fixtures, a marble lobby, and the latest office equipment. It housed 235 officers and employees when it opened in 1931. Although Hazel-Atlas did not manufacture glass in Wheeling, the company did make jar lids, including those for popular products such as Jif Peanut Butter, Maxwell House Coffee, and French's Mustard. The Jacob Street building was donated to West Liberty State College in 1966 (pictured here), and in 1972, it became the home of West Virginia Northern Community College. It is now owned by the Youth Services System. (WVNCC Alumni Association.)

Travel south on Jacob Street to Seventeenth Street and make a left. Near the east end of Seventeenth Street, access the Wheeling Heritage Trail that follows the path of the former B&O train tracks. Cross the Hempfield Viaduct spanning Wheeling Creek to the Hempfield Railroad Tunnel. The beautiful stone-arch viaduct was designed by Charles Ellet Jr., the same man who designed Wheeling's suspension bridge. Just before entering the tunnel, a wooded path to the right leads to an infamous Wheeling landmark known as Wetzel's Cave. Lewis Wetzel was a rugged frontiersman who, according to legend, killed a Native American who used the cave to set up ambushes. Walk along the path another 125 feet to visit the larger shelter cave, where naturalist A. B. Brooks (seated, with cane) was photographed with one of his nature excursion groups in the early 20th century. (Then, Museums of Oglebay Institute; Now, Seán Duffy.)

Return to Seventeenth Street and follow it west to Chapline Street. Head south, past the Ohio Valley Medical Center, and go left on Twenty-second Street. At the top of the hill is an old bridge (now closed to traffic) over West Virginia Route 2. Walk the bridge to the hillside for this dramatic view of Wheeling. The historic photograph, taken in the 1930s, offers a good view of the Pollack Stogie Factory on Eighteenth and Eoff Streets. Augustus Pollack founded the company in 1871, and the Eighteenth Street factory was built in 1909. Wholesale hardware company Ott-Heiskell bought the building in 1956. Also visible in the left background is the 1907 Schmulbach Building, now owned by Severstal North America. Other significant structures visible include the Scottish Rite Cathedral (right), St. Joseph's Cathedral (center), and the old and new city-county buildings (left center). (Ellen Dunable.)

Go back down the old bridge to the Ohio Valley Medical Center (OVMC). Founded in 1890 as City Hospital, OVMC was known as Ohio Valley General Hospital when, in 1959, a young woman named Ann Prince Thomas became the first African American to graduate from the hospital's school of nursing. A true pioneer and witness to history, Thomas grew up as Wheeling transitioned from a fully segregated town (where she attended Lincoln School) to a desegregated one (where she graduated from Wheeling High School). But even after America's high court finally rejected Jim Crow laws, Thomas remembers a restaurant refusing to serve her as she celebrated with her classmates. And when she traveled to Charleston to take her licensing exam, she had to stay with family friends because the hotel refused her a room. But she persevered, passed her exam, and worked as a registered nurse for 40 years. (Ann Thomas.)

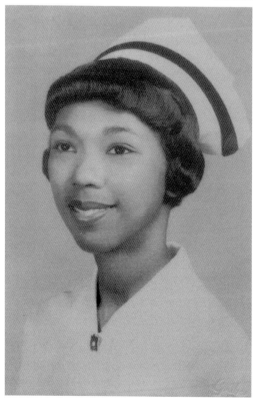

From the hospital, follow Twenty-second Street west back to Market Street. Travel two blocks north to see the Bennett Square Building at 2100 Market Street. In 1904, Wheeling's city fathers attempted to pass a bond levy in order to acquire a Carnegie Free Library, like hundreds of other cities across America had done. But Wheeling was the most unionized city in West Virginia, and the violence perpetrated by the Pinkerton guards hired by Pittsburgh industrialist Andrew Carnegie to protect scabs during the 1892 Homestead Strike was still a fresh wound on the psyche of Wheeling's workers. Labor interests in Wheeling organized against the proposed library, the voters defeated the levy, and Wheeling became the first American city to reject a Carnegie Library. In 1911, the Wheeling library got its own building, designed by Charles W. Bates at 2100 Market Street. In 1973, a new Ohio County Public Library opened at 52 Sixteenth Street on the site of the old power plant for the B&O passenger station. (West Virginia State Archives.)

Follow Market Street south past Wheeling's historic Centre Market to Twenty-third Street. Go left on Twenty-third Street a few blocks to the intersection with Chapline Street and look to the southeast corner, where this distinctive 1870 Second Empire–style residence still stands. The historic photograph was taken during the 1906 Saengerfest parade. The decorated wagon reads "Jos. Speidel Grocery Co." Speidel operated a large wholesale grocery business on Main Street near Fourteenth Street. According to a note with the photograph, "That's Winifred [Stifel] on curb at left." Note the policeman with his bobby helmet and nightstick. (Dr. Dennis Niess.)

Look to the southwest corner of Chapline and Twenty-third Streets for this final image in the 1906 Saengerfest parade series. This 1889 Queen Anne–style residence is also still standing and is the first house in Chapline Street Row, a much-photographed set of homes that have been called the best extant example of a series of high Victorian structures in West Virginia. Notes included with the photographs indicate that Elizabeth and Laura Stifel were aboard this buggy. According to the late Wheeling historian Edward Wolf, the parade, which included all of the 24 regional singing societies in attendance, as well as several bands, "ended in South Wheeling where everyone then took the incline for a mammoth picnic at Mozart Park." Such a finale no doubt pleased Henry Schmulbach (see page 77). (Dr. Dennis Niess.)

Follow Chapline Street to Thirty-first Street in South Wheeling, take a left on Thirty-first Street, and proceed to the Wood Street intersection. Once the leading producer of cut nails in the nation, Wheeling earned the title "Nail City," and La Belle Nailworks, founded in 1852, was Wheeling's leading nail producer. Today La Belle provides Wheeling's most impressive industrial survival story. It is one of only two operating cut nail factories in the United States, supplying steel nails for both construction and historic restoration projects, including, in 1991, Thomas Jefferson's Monticello. Current owner Denis McMorrow of Atlanta has worked hard to keep La Belle's doors open. The historic photograph features a hand-forged iron sign created by a La Belle blacksmith a century or more ago hanging above the door of the cooperage. On a visit in January 2010, the cooperage was long gone, but current blacksmith Jodi Parsons and manager John Osmianski found the old sign stashed away in a dusty corner. Jodi mounted the sign using La Belle-made masonry nails for this photo op. (West Virginia State Archives.)

Travel back to Jacob Street and follow it to Thirty-third Street. Businessman Henry Schmulbach acquired Nail City Brewery at Thirty-third and Wetzel Streets in 1881. Schmulbach produced a lager that, according to the *Wheeling Daily Intelligencer*, had "its votaries who pronounce it the best beer made." Schmulbach cut storage caves into the hillside and built, on Forty-third Street, a funicular railway to his beer garden at Mozart Park, where the final celebration of the 1906 Saengerfest took place. Although key buildings were razed to make way for West Virginia Route 2 in the 1970s, a few structures still stand and provide fine examples of 19th-century brewery architecture. Like most of Wheeling's breweries, Schmulbach was put out of business by state prohibition in 1914. (Albert Doughty Jr.)

Go back to Jacob Street and follow it south to Thirty-sixth Street. Cooey-Bentz Company was a South Wheeling stalwart and a one-stop shop for funeral services, furniture, and dry goods at the corner of Jacob and Thirty-sixth Streets. Undertaker W. R. Cooey and cooper Herman Bentz expanded several times, most notably in 1923, when architect Frederick Faris joined with the R. R. Kitchen Company to build the new five-story addition seen here. Cooey-Bentz served as a temporary morgue, storing dozens of bodies after the horrific Benwood Mine explosion of 1924 (see page 89). During the 1970s and early 1980s, Cooey-Bentz developed into a Yuletide mecca, featuring a sprawling toyland with a huge toy train display, eye-catching animated window displays, and the most popular Santa Claus in the region. Cooey-Bentz closed in 2002. (Jeff Knierim.)

CHAPTER 4

OUT THE PIKE

Moses Shepherd and Lydia Boggs both assisted in the defense of Fort Henry against Native American attackers. They later married, residing in the Stone House, built in 1798 along National Road in what is now Elm Grove. The Shepherds were friends of U.S. senator Henry Clay, who helped ensure that the new National Road was constructed to pass directly by the Shepherd plantation. To show their gratitude, the Shepherds commissioned a monument to Clay to be erected on their property, which subsequently became known as Monument Place. Seen here in 1888, Monument Place is now home to the Osiris Shrine Temple. (Brown collection, OCPL.)

From South Wheeling, return to Market Street. In the 19th century, as Wheeling's business class prospered, it was common for wealthier residents to leave the city and move "Out the Pike," meaning east on National Road, to estates in Woodlawn, Edgewood, and Pleasant Valley. Market Street north of Tenth Street is part of the Old Pike. To get the full flavor of the migration, follow it over Wheeling Hill, where Samuel McColloch made his leap, through Fulton and on to the junction with Bethany Pike, where Frank Walters's Two-Mile House (pictured here in 1888) once sat, providing beer and rest for weary travelers. The lovely Romanesque Vance Memorial Presbyterian Church was built on the site by Wheeling businessman James Nelson Vance in 1897 in memory of his parents. (Brown collection, OCPL.)

The large fields of Woodlawn, located just east of Bethany Pike near Vance Memorial Church, were a perfect campground for National Guard troops, seen here drilling around 1900, as well-dressed onlookers observe the action. The fields are now part of the Woodsdale residential area. (Then, Dr. Dennis Niess; Now, Seán Duffy.)

Continue east on National Road about half a mile over Chicken Neck Hill and turn left onto Edgington Lane. Proceed a few blocks to the intersection of Edgington Lane and Carmel Road, seen here in 1908. The scene has changed rather dramatically, but it still retains its suburban charm. (Emmerth family.)

Turn left on Carmel Road. The Ye Olde Alpha is on the right. Arguably Wheeling's most beloved surviving watering hole, the Alpha began life as the Alpha Vaudeville/Nickelodeon Theatre in 1913, promising first-class pictures every evening. After being converted to the Alpha Beer Garden in the early 1930s, Frank Miller (pictured in the 1950s) opened a restaurant at the location in 1938. The name was changed to Ye Olde Alpha in 1941. The "dead animals" for which the Alpha is famous were collected over the years by Miller on hunting trips to Idaho and other locales. The trademark moose was mounted in 1955. Current owners Mark Thomas and Charlie Schlegel (pictured) continue to honor the Alpha tradition while adding a modern flair. (Ron Miller.)

Return to National Road and continue east. One half-block from Edgington Lane on the left sits the distinctive, Spanish mission–style El Villa apartment building, seen here in the 1930s. Designed by prolific architect Edward Bates Franzheim, the El Villa stands out amid the consistently Victorian and Edwardian architecture of Edgewood. (West Virginia State Archives.)

Two blocks east on the Old Pike sits a splendid Queen Anne–style mansion just across from St. Michael's School and Church. Built in 1891 by Mail Pouch Tobacco founder Samuel S. Bloch, the mansion, known as Elmhurst, served as the Bloch family residence until 1940, when the family donated the estate to the Home for Aged Women. A new wing was added to the House of Friendship in 1942. The retirement home currently houses 39 residents, both men and women. (*Art Work of Wheeling*, 1904, OCPL.)

Make a right on Washington Avenue and follow it to the Mount de Chantal entrance just before the Interstate 70 on-ramp. The Visitation Sisters of Baltimore, at the invitation of Bishop Richard Whelan, founded Mount de Chantal Academy for girls in April 1848. The building, pictured in the 1890s, was finished just after the Civil War and houses two magnificent chandeliers made by Wheeling's Hobbs-Brockunier glass company. Mount de Chantal gained a national reputation for excellence. Graduates included young ladies from prominent local families such as the McLures, Reymanns, Stifels, and Zanes. The academy graduated its last class in 2008. Sadly, as this book was being produced, plans were being made for the building to be sold, while the remaining Visitation Sisters were scheduled to relocate to the Georgetown Monastery in Washington, D.C. (Mount de Chantal Archives.)

Take Washington Avenue back to National Road and head east. Stop just before reaching Mount Calvary Cemetery on the left for this 1885 view of the Old Pike when it was still an unpaved road frequented by stagecoaches and pedestrians. Note the trolley tracks crossing the road in the historic photograph. Pleasant Valley remains one of the most beautiful sections of Wheeling. (Brown collection, OCPL.)

Make a left into Mount Calvary Cemetery at 1685 National Road. On April 28, 1924, an explosion in a Benwood coal mine killed 119 men, mostly Italian and Polish immigrants. On May 5, 1924, twenty-two of the deceased were buried side by side at Mount Calvary, Wheeling's primary Catholic cemetery. It was the largest mass burial Wheeling had ever experienced. The service was conducted in English, Polish, and Italian. The priest in the center of the photograph was a Benwood man, Fr. P. M. Schoenen. The names on the tombstones pictured include Kuprewicz, DiGiorgio, Ferri, Piechowicz, Pirrera, Dupla, Dlugoborski, Malyska, Kazemka, Rea, Shalayka, Staszewski, and Kopetz. (Then, Diocese of Wheeling-Charleston; Now, Seán Duffy.)

From the cemetery, turn left on National Road and travel a short distance to the entrance of Wheeling Park, once the residence of Thomas Hornbrook and later sold to a group led by brewer Anton Reymann. It then functioned as a sort of German beer garden and private amusement park, featuring a roller coaster and a casino, where international megastar Sarah Bernhardt appeared in 1905. The old gate pictured was built in the early 20th century, when the park was the last stop on Wheeling's streetcar line. The land was acquired by the city in 1924 and was opened as a public park a year later. The Sonneborn Gates, designed by Edward Bates Franzheim, replaced the old gate in the 1920s. (Ellen Dunable.)

Continue east to Elm Grove, stopping at 2167 National Road. In this 1940s photograph, an old steam locomotive chugs out of the Elm Grove B&O Station, belching coal soot. Once a common sight, sound, and smell, the steam train is now a dinosaur in Wheeling. The elevated track spanning National Road that brought trains like this one into the Elm Grove station has long since been removed, and the building now houses a landscaping business. (J. J. Young collection, WVNCC Alumni Association.)

Just east of the old railroad station stands the oldest bridge in West Virginia. This three-span elliptical stone arch spanning Wheeling Creek on National Road was built by Col. Moses Shepherd in 1817. Perhaps to satisfy his wife, Lydia's, vanity, Shepherd used his influence with Senator Henry Clay to change the location of the bridge so the National Road would run nearer to the Shepherd estate. Shepherd built a monument to Clay nearby, and the bridge is sometimes known as the Monument Place Bridge. Unfortunately, its beautiful limestone building blocks were covered in concrete in 1958. For this view, bring some wading gear. (Brown collection, OCPL.)

Shortly after midnight on July 29, 1945, the U.S. Navy cruiser *Indianapolis* was en route to the Philippines, having just delivered components of the atomic bomb later dropped on Hiroshima. Paul W. McGinnis of Wheeling, a 19-year-old off-duty signalman, was awakened by a violent explosion. The *Indianapolis* had been struck by two Japanese torpedoes and sank in just minutes. McGinnis and the others who made it off the ship spent five horrific days adrift—starving, thirsty, and relentlessly harassed by sharks. Of the 1,196 crew, perhaps 900 made it into the water, and only 317 survived. Amazingly, although he witnessed the fear and carnage they caused, McGinnis says he never saw a shark. Here McGinnis poses shortly after being rescued and, 69 years later, strikes a similar pose just outside his Bethlehem home. He now spends his days relaxing with his wife, Marcella, or working in his woodshop. (Paul McGinnis.)

Continue east on the Old Pike through Triadelphia and on to Roney's Point. The Valley Camp Coal Company once owned numerous mines in the Wheeling area. Miners were often paid in scrip that could only be redeemed in company stores like this one. Valley Camp Store No. 3 was located along National Road in Triadelphia near Roney's Point. In this pre–World War II photograph, the third driver from the left is H. E. "Tiny" Timmons, the father of Gary Timmons, who shared the photograph. The building now houses the Ohio Valley Baptist Church. (Gary Timmons.)

A few miles east sits one of the oldest surviving structures in the Wheeling area. The Old Stone House at Roney's Point was built prior to 1828. As a tavern, it served stagecoach passengers on the National Road and was "a lively place during the palmy days of the road," according to Thomas Searight's *The Old Pike*. Originally operated by Ninian Bell, the tavern was constructed with hand-cut local stone. The Stone House was said to be a popular stop for young romanticists traveling west. (Gary Timmons.)

94

The last stop on this tour of historic Wheeling is a sad one. This mansion, built in 1913 by businessman Henry Schmulbach on his farmland at Roney's Point, still looks beautiful in the 1930s photograph. Some years after Schmulbach died, Ohio County purchased the estate, using the mansion as a poor farm and adding a tuberculosis sanitarium. Later the state built a mental health facility just up the road. By the late 1960s, the mansion was abandoned, and urban legends about the property rendered it a popular drinking destination for teenagers. Fires and vandalism did the rest. The once-magnificent residence is now a sad ruin. (Gary Timmons.)

DISCOVER THOUSANDS OF LOCAL HISTORY BOOKS
FEATURING MILLIONS OF VINTAGE IMAGES

Arcadia Publishing, the leading local history publisher in the United States, is committed to making history accessible and meaningful through publishing books that celebrate and preserve the heritage of America's people and places.

Find more books like this at
www.arcadiapublishing.com

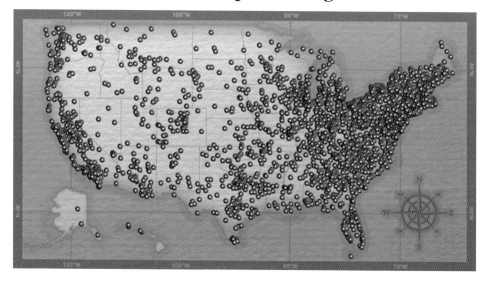

Search for your hometown history, your old stomping grounds, and even your favorite sports team.

Consistent with our mission to preserve history on a local level, this book was printed in South Carolina on American-made paper and manufactured entirely in the United States. Products carrying the accredited Forest Stewardship Council (FSC) label are printed on 100 percent FSC-certified paper.

MADE IN THE USA